Kids'
COOKBOOK

JG
PRESS

Published by World Publications Group, Inc.
140 Laurel Street
East Bridgewater, MA 02333
www.wrldpub.net

10 9 8 7 6 5 4 3 2 1

ISBN 13: 978-1-57215-465-0
ISBN 10: 1-57215-465-9

Project Managed by Kandour

Editorial and design management: Emma Hayley and Jenny Ross
Author: James Mitchell
Design and layout: Kurt Young
Cover design: Paul Barton
Editor: Josephine Bacon
Photography: CEPHAS / StockFood;
CEPHAS / Vince Hart (page 32); Photos.com

Printed in China.

Contents

Before you start

Cooking is great fun but, with lots of hot and sharp things around, it can also be dangerous. Make sure you read these simple rules and follow them every time you are in the kitchen, so as to be safe, and the food you cook will be delicious.

The Rules

1 NEVER COOK ANYTHING WITHOUT AN ADULT THERE TO HELP YOU.

2 Always ask a grownup to help you with anything sharp, hot, or electrical, and don't be afraid to ask questions, even the best chefs ask for help.

3 Before you start cooking, always give your hands a good wash with soap and clean the work surfaces.

4 When you're using a knife, be very careful, and always use a chopping board. Hold the knife firmly, point the blade downward, and keep your fingers out of the way.

5 Whenever you need to move something hot, always use oven gloves or a pot-holder. Anything hot can give you a nasty burn, so it's better to get a grownup to handle the hot stuff for you. If you burn yourself, run the cold faucet on the burn straight away and continue for at least ten minutes. It will feel really, really cold, but it's worth it because the burn won't sting later.

6 Make sure the handles of saucepans aren't sticking out from the stovetop or work surface so no one can knock against them. That goes for the grownups too!

7 Make sure you have dry hands before you touch anything electrical, such as plugs, sockets, and household appliances. If your hands are wet, you could give yourself an electric shock.

8 Keep a clean cloth nearby and wipe up anything you spill straight away, especially if it's on the floor.

9 Hot pans should always be placed on a heatproof mat or stand.

10 Bacteria are everywhere in the world and sometimes food can have some on it that might make you sick. Always wash fruits and vegetables before you use them and wash your hands, knife, and chopping board when you've been touching raw fish or meat. Always clean up and tidy up as you work.

11 **Making sure your food tastes great!** Read the recipe all the way through before you shop for the ingredients and before you start cooking. Make a shopping list, then get a grownup to check it for you, because you might have some of the ingredients already.

12 Take extra care weighing and measuring ingredients. If you rush this, it's easy for your recipe to go wrong. Make sure you have a set of measuring cups, spoons, and preferably a weigh-scale too.

13 Don't rush: it's better for the food to be a little late than for it not to taste good. If you put love and care into your cooking, it actually makes the food taste better!

14 **Finally the most important rule of all—HAVE FUN!**

Watch out for:
lb means pound
oz means ounce

Peanut Butter & Banana Shake

Makes 1 shake

This is a quick milkshake for your breakfast. It will give you loads of energy for the morning!

You will need:
A blender

Ingredients

1 banana

1 heaping tablespoon smooth peanut butter

1/2 cup milk

To decorate (optional):
Whipped cream and candied cherries

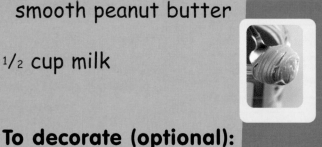

1 Before you go to bed, peel and chop the banana into bite-size pieces.

2 Put it in a plastic bag and leave in the freezer overnight.

3 When you wake up, put all the ingredients in the blender, get a grownup to help you with this, and whiz it up for about a minute, or until it's really thick and smooth. Make sure you hold the lid down when you switch on the blender or your shake might end up all over the kitchen!

Extras!
Try swapping the peanut butter for one of these:

1/4 cup strawberries, blueberries, or raspberries, and a teaspoon of liquid honey

1 heaping tablespoon sweetened cocoa powder

Scrumbled Eggs

Feeds 1

This is a real easy recipe that everyone likes!

You'll need:
A small mixing bowl
A toaster
A nonstick saucepan
A wooden spoon

Ingredients

2 free-range eggs

2 slices of bread

A dash of salt

1 stick butter

To decorate (optional):
Chopped chives

Extras!
For something a little more special, add:
- 4 tablespoons grated cheese with
      4 tablespoons chopped ham
- 4 tablespoons chopped smoked salmon (lox)
- 1 frank or wiener, chopped

Just add any of these to the eggs when you turn off the heat and give it all a good stir with the wooden spoon.

1 Crack the eggs into a bowl, add the salt, and beat with a fork.

2 Next, put the bread in the toaster ready to toast.

3 Heat 1 tablespoon of the butter in the saucepan over a medium heat. When the butter has melted, press the bread down in the toaster. Then pour the beaten eggs into the melted butter and start stirring them with a wooden spoon. The secret of good scrambled eggs is to keep mixing the eggs all the time and to make sure you get the spoon right into the corners and edges of the pan, mixing in any bits that are sticking.

4 When the eggs are creamy and still slightly liquid, turn off the heat. They'll keep cooking by themselves for a little longer.

5 Butter your toast, which should be ready by now, and either serve the eggs on top of it or on the side.

8

Cinnamon French Toast

Feeds 1

Sweet and delicious, this is a great alternative to plain old toast!

You'll need:
A small mixing bowl
A nonstick skillet
A metal spatula
Oven gloves
An apron

Ingredients

1 free-range egg

²/₃ cup milk

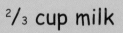

2 tablespoons brown sugar

2 tablespoons powdered cinnamon

2 thick slices white bread

Butter for frying

1 Break the egg into the bowl. Add the milk, sugar, and cinnamon, and beat with a fork until it's well mixed.

2 Next, soak the bread slices in the egg mixture. Make sure they are completely covered.

3 Put on your oven gloves and apron. Get a grownup to help you heat your skillet to a medium heat and add around half a teaspoonful of butter. When the butter has melted and has started to foam, add in your soaked bread and fry until it is golden-brown underneath. You can check this by carefully lifting up the end with the metal spatula. Flip the bread slices over with the metal spatula and fry them on the other side.

Extras!
Try regular French toast, which is also yummy. Leave out the sugar and cinnamon, and then serve it with some Canadian bacon or baked beans. You can also add strips of orange zest to the egg mixture, as in the picture.

Pancake Pals

Makes 4 pancake pals

This recipe is great for you to make for the family at the weekends or if you have friends to sleep over!

You'll need:
A blender
A skillet
A ladle
A metal spatula
An apron

Ingredients

2 cups all-purpose flour

3 teaspoons baking powder

A dash of salt

2 teaspoons vegetable oil plus extra for frying

1³/₄ cups milk

2 free-range eggs

12 blueberries

2 strawberries, cut in half

Maple syrup for serving

1 First preheat the oven to the lowest setting.

2 Put on your apron and get a grownup to help you with this. Using electrical appliances and cooking can be dangerous as the skillet and oil will be very hot, so never try this on your own.

3 Put everything apart from the blueberries, strawberries, and maple syrup in the blender. Cover with the lid, and whiz it all for a minute until it's all mixed up and smooth. Don't forget to hold on the lid before you switch on the blender or you'll be wearing your breakfast!

4 Heat the skillet to a medium heat and add half a teaspoon of oil, then pour a ladle of pancake mix in the center of the skillet for the face and then pour two little bits for the ears. When bubbles start to appear in the center of your pancake, flip it over with the metal spatula and cook for another minute, or until both sides are golden-brown.

5 Put the pancake on a plate and ask a grownup to put it in the oven while you make the rest.

6 When you've cooked the four pancakes, put them on plates and decorate them. Add half a strawberry for the mouth and blueberries for the eyes and nose.

7 Serve with the maple syrup poured around the edge.

Extras!
Try adding 1/2 cup blueberries to the pancake mix before cooking the pancakes, or serve each pancake with two slices of broiled lean Canadian bacon.

Oatmeal and Fruit Breakfast

Makes 2 servings

This is good because you do all the hard work before bedtime and when you're sleepy in the morning your yummy breakfast is already made!

You'll need:
A medium mixing bowl
A cheese-grater

Ingredients

$1^1/_3$ cups raw oatmeal

1 green dessert apple

$^2/_3$ cup plain yogurt

$^1/_3$ cup milk

2 teaspoons liquid honey or maple syrup

1 Put the oatmeal, milk, yogurt, and honey in the mixing bowl.

2 Next cut the apple into quarters and cut out the core. Then grate the apple, without peeling it and mix it into the mixing bowl before it turns brown. Give it all a really good stir and then cover it with some plastic wrap and refrigerate it ready for the morning.

3 When you wake up in the morning, share the mixture between two bowls, and then choose two or three of the following ingredients to put into each bowl:
2 tablespoons chopped nuts
2 tablespoons currants, raisins, or any other dried fruits
2 tablespoons raspberries, blueberries, or chopped up strawberries
$^1/_2$ chopped up banana, 1 tablespoon apples shaped like stars, and pieces of chopped orange.

Gooey Chocolate Brownies

Makes 12-15 brownies

These lovely chocolate brownies are chewy and squidgy in the center!

You'll need:
An 8-inch square baking pan
Microwave oven or a
  large saucepan
A large mixing bowl
A wooden spoon
A sieve
A metal spatula
Oven gloves
A wire cooling rack

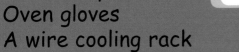

Ingredients

Extra butter for greasing
  the pan
2 squares dark baking
  chocolate
1 stick butter, softened
1 teaspoon vanilla extract
1 cup of sugar
2 free-range eggs
4 tablespoons
  all-purpose flour
A dash of salt
1/2 teaspoon
  baking powder

1 Preheat the oven to: 350°F and grease the baking pan with butter.

2 Break up the chocolate and put it in the mixing bowl. Microwave it for 2 minutes on the defrost setting or until it has all melted. If you don't have a microwave oven, get a grownup to heat about 2 inches of water in a large saucepan until it's steaming, and then put the mixing bowl on top to melt the chocolate.

3 Next mix in the butter, vanilla extract, and sugar into the melted chocolate, beating with a wooden spoon. When the mixture is smooth, beat the eggs, and stir them in. Sift the flour, salt, and baking powder into the bowl and beat the mixture until smooth. Pour the mixture into the greased baking pan and spread it out to the corners, using the metal spatula.

Extras!
Try adding 4 tablespoons chocolate chips, raisins, or chopped nuts to the mixture at stage 3.

4 Get a grownup to put the pan in the center of the oven and bake the mixture for 25 to 30 minutes, or until the edges are firm, but the cake is springy in the center.

5 Let the pan cool down for 15 minutes then cut it into 12 to 15 squares using the metal spatula. Arrange the brownies on the wire cooling rack and leave them to cool.

Gingerbread People

Makes 15–20 people

"Run, run as fast as you can! You can't catch me I'm
the Gingerbread Man!"

You'll need:

A sieve
A large mixing bowl
A saucepan
A wooden spoon
A rolling pin
Gingerbread people
   cookie cutters
A cookie sheet
A metal spatula
A wire cooling rack
A piping bag or a
   plastic freezer bag

Ingredients

2 cups all-purpose flour
1 teaspoon baking powder
2 teaspoons ground ginger
$\frac{1}{2}$ cup butter, softened
$\frac{1}{3}$ cup soft brown sugar
2 tablespoons dark corn syrup

To decorate (optional):

1 cup confectioner's
sugar; currants or
pieces of candied cherry

1 Preheat the oven to 350°F. Sift
the flour, baking powder, and ginger
into a mixing bowl.

2 Ask a grownup to melt the butter,
sugar, and dark corn syrup in a
saucepan. Let the mixture cool for
a few minutes and then pour into
the flour mixture. Stir it with a
wooden spoon and then knead it into
a big ball with your hands.

3 Dust a work surface and rolling pin
with a little flour and then roll the
dough out until it's about 1/4 inch
thick. Use the cookie cutter to cut
out the people. If you have any
dough left, roll it out again and cut
out a couple more.

4 Transfer the people to a cookie
sheet using a metal spatula. Ask a
grownup to bake them in the center
of the oven for 10 to 12 minutes,
until they are golden-brown.

5 Let them cool down for a few
minutes and then move them to a
wire rack to cool.

6 For the frosting, sift the confectioner's sugar into a bowl, add a tablespoon of water, and mix it together. Spoon it into a piping bag or a freezer bag with the tip of a corner snipped off, and draw faces and clothes on your people.

7 You can push currants or little pieces of candied cherry into your cookies for eyes and buttons.

Chocolate Cruckles

Makes about 15 crackles

Everyone loves these crunchy little chocolate treats.
Make sure you keep them away from the grownups!

You'll need:

A mixing bowl

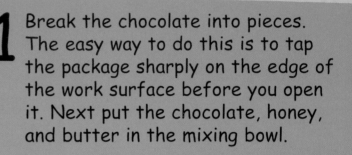

Microwave oven or
a large saucepan

A wooden spoon

15 paper cupcake cases

Ingredients:

$2/3$ cup chocolate (milk,
white, or dark, whichever
you like best)

1 tablespoon liquid honey

4 tablespoons butter

$1^1/3$ cups cornflakes

Extras!

Try using different types of breakfast
cereal, such as Rice Crispies, or add
2 tablespoons raisins or chopped nuts
to the chocolate.

1 Break the chocolate into pieces.
The easy way to do this is to tap
the package sharply on the edge of
the work surface before you open
it. Next put the chocolate, honey,
and butter in the mixing bowl.

2 Put the bowl in the microwave oven
on the defrost setting and cook
for 2 minutes, or until the
chocolate has melted.

3 If you don't have a microwave oven,
get a grownup to heat about 2
inches of water in a large saucepan
until it's steaming, then put the
mixing bowl on top to melt the
chocolate.

4 Stir the mixture with a wooden
spoon until it's smooth and then
carefully stir in the cornflakes so
they are completely covered with
the melted chocolate.

5 Spoon a tablespoon of the mixture
into each of the paper cupcake
cases, leave to cool to room
temperature, and then put them in
the refrigerator to set.

Banana Split

Makes 1

Banana Split has been eaten for years and everyone still loves it!

You'll need:
A plastic knife
An ice cream scoop

Ingredients

1 banana
2 scoops ice cream or
  frozen yogurt

Fixings:

Chocolate, raspberry, or strawberry sauce

Strawberries, raspberries, blueberries, cherries, or grapes

Chopped nuts, sprinkles, or chocolate chips

1 Peel the banana and then slice it down the center lengthwise. Arrange the banana in a sundae glass and put 2 scoops of ice cream on top of it.

2 Cover your banana split with lots of fixings!

Icy Poles

Why spend lots of money on popsicles at the store when you can make nicer ones at home? You can buy really inexpensive popsicle-making kits from cookware stores. Why not save up your pocket money and buy a set? You'll make great savings in the long run!

You'll need:
A set of popsicle molds

Ingredients

Juices: Orange, apple, grape, pineapple, cranberry, or a mixture.
Smoothies: strawberry, mango, blueberry.
Syrup: Blackcurrant, orange, lemon.
Soda pop: Lemonade, cola, cream soda.

1 This is so easy you could do it with your eyes closed! All you need to do is fill up the molds with some of your favorite drinks above and put them in the freezer until they are completely frozen. Be careful to pour any soda pop slowly, as it will fizz up!

Peanut Butter Cookies

Makes about 36 cookies

These peanut butter cookies are great to share. Why not take some to class to share with your friends?

You'll need:

A large mixing bowl

A wooden spoon

A fork

A sieve

A large nonstick or greased cookie sheet

Oven gloves

A wire cooling rack

Ingredients

$2/3$ cup soft butter

$2/3$ cup smooth peanut butter

1 teaspoon vanilla extract

$1^1/4$ cups packed soft brown sugar

2 free-range eggs

2 cups all-purpose flour

1 teaspoon baking powder

$1/2$ teaspoon salt

1 Preheat the oven to: 350°F.

2 Put the butter, peanut butter, vanilla extract, and sugar into the mixing bowl and beat together. Next, beat the eggs with a fork, and then beat them into the mixture.

3 Sift the flour, baking powder, and salt into the peanut butter mixture, and mix together until the mixture is smooth.

4 Drop tablespoons of the mixture onto the cookie sheet. You don't have to spread them out. Then get a grownup to put them in the oven for you. Bake for 10 minutes if you like them chewy, or for 15 minutes if you like them crispy.

5 Let the cookies cool on the cookie sheet for 5 minutes and then move them to a wire rack to cool down completely.

Extras!

Try adding $1/2$ cup chopped raw peanuts or chocolate chips to the mixture, or arrange peanuts and chocolate on the top of the cookies to look like faces.

Sticky Chicken Wings

Feeds 4

The best food is stuff you can eat with your fingers.
These are great for a snack or as fun party food!

You'll need:
A mixing bowl
A fork
A baking tray
Oven gloves
Kitchen tongs

Ingredients

2 tablespoons olive
or sunflower oil

2 tablespoons fresh
orange juice

2 tablespoons soy sauce

2 tablespoons liquid honey

$^1/_2$ teaspoon smoked paprika

1 garlic clove, minced

12 chicken wings

1 Put everything apart from the chicken wings in a bowl and mix them together with a fork.

2 Then add the chicken wings and stir them around until they are completely coated in the sauce. Cover the bowl with plastic wrap and refrigerate it for 1 to 2 hours, to marinate. That means all the flavors will get into the chicken.

3 When you're ready to cook them, preheat the oven to 400°F.

4 Put the wings on a baking tray and pour the rest of the sauce over them. Get a grownup to put them in the center of the oven to bake for 15 minutes.

5 After 15 minutes, ask a grownup to take them out of the oven and turn them over with a pair of tongs. If you're careful, you can help with this, but make sure you're with a grownup and watch out for the hot baking tray!

6 Then put them back in the oven for another 15 minutes.

7 When they are ready, make sure you've got lots of paper towels to wipe your sticky fingers!

Extras!

Try swapping the honey for maple syrup. Also, when you're turning over the wings after 15 minutes, try sprinkling them with 2 tablespoons of sesame seeds to coat them all over.

Garlic Bread

Makes 1 loaf

Eating lots of garlic can make your breath smell a bit the next day, so makes sure that everyone eats some, and then none of you will notice!

You'll need:
A garlic press
A serrated plastic knife
A chopping board
A butter knife
A small bowl
Some aluminum foil
Oven gloves

Ingredients

1 French stick

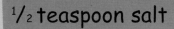

1 stick soft butter

4 garlic cloves, crushed

¹/₂ teaspoon salt

1 Preheat the oven to: 350°F.

2 Mix together the garlic, butter, and salt in the bowl.

3 Now put the French stick on the chopping board and get a grownup to help you cut into it with a plastic knife. The slices should be about 1 inch wide, but stop about ¹/₂ inch from the bottom so the French stick is still joined up.

4 Use the butter knife to spread the garlic butter between all of the cuts and then push the French stick back together again.

5 Wrap the French stick loosely in aluminum foil, scrunching the ends together so it's sealed up. Then get a grownup to put it in the oven, where it must bake for 25 minutes.

6 When a grownup has taken it out of the oven, let it cool down for 2 minutes then carefully unwrap the aluminum foil, because it will be very hot inside. Now it's ready to eat!

28

Extras!

For cheesy garlic bread, try inserting $1/2$ cup grated yellow cheese into the cuts before baking the bread. Or for herby garlic bread, try mixing a tablespoon of freshly chopped herbs such as rosemary, parsley, or thyme into the butter.

Smiley Sandwiches

Makes 2

These are like paintings that you can eat and you can make them different every time. The faces can be decorated with any ingredients you have in the kitchen, just check with a grownup before you use them.

Ingredients

6 tablespoons small-curd cottage cheese

2 slices of bread

Alfalfa sprouts

Paprika

Slices of radish or jicama

Slices of bell pepper

Strips and slices of cucumbers

Salsa

1 Spread the cottage cheese over the slices of bread.

2 Sprinkle some alfalfa at the top of the slice for hair and dust a little paprika across the center for red cheeks.

3 For the eyes, use two slices of radish or jicama with a dot of salsa in the center, then for eyebrows use two strips of cucumber.
For the nose use a little triangle of cucumber and for the mouth a slice of bell pepper.

Snake Stick

Feeds 6

This is an exsssselent sssssnack to make for friendssssss!

You'll need:
A serrated plastic knife
A chopping board
A butter knife
2 cocktail sticks

Ingredients

1 red bell pepper

1 French stick

Butter

12 slices salami
  or pepperoni

A few lettuce leaves,
  shredded

2 olives (stuffed with
  red bell pepper)

Tomato ketchup

Extras!
You can try filling your snake with other
ingredients. Slices of cheese, ham,
cucumber, tomato—anything you want!

1 Cut the bell pepper in half and scrape out the seeds and white parts with a spoon. Then slice it, saving a strip for the tongue. To make the tongue, just cut a V in one end.

2 Next, cut the French stick in half lengthwise through the center and butter the lower half, using the butter knife. Layer the strips of pepper over the butter, then add layers of salami and lettuce. Finally, put the top half of the French stick over the lower half, and push down firmly.

3 Next, to make the face of your snake, poke the tongue out of one end of the French stick, and stick on the olives with the cocktail sticks for its eyes.

4 Chop the French stick into sections and arrange the pieces in an S-shape like a snake. To make its markings, squeeze a zigzag strip of tomato ketchup along its back.

Have fun with veg!

Try having fun with vegetables.
Take a serrated plastic knife and
chop, carve, and shape vegetables
into various cute animals and items.
Use a cocktail stick and cream
cheese to stick bits together.
It's like having an art class in
the kitchen!

Stringy Nachos

Feeds 2

This is a super-quick snack to make when you're hungry.

You'll need:
A plastic serrated knife
A spoon
A chopping board
A cheese-grater

Ingredients

1 red bell pepper
10 slices jalapeño pepper
(if you like it hot!)
10 black olives, pitted
²/₃ cup grated Cheddar,
American, or Jack cheese

1 package tortilla chips

Extras!
Try putting other things on top of
the tortilla chips, such as chopped
tomato, thinly sliced Bermuda onion,
or chunks of avocado. If you've got
some salsa or guacamole in the
refrigerator you can put that on
top too.

1 Preheat the broiler to high. Cut the bell peppers in half and scrape out the seeds and white parts with a spoon, then chop them into small pieces. Combine the jalapeño peppers –make sure you wash your hands after this, and don't touch your eyes because the jalapeño will make them sting! Then slice up the olives.

2 Get a grownup to grate the cheese coarsely, using the large holes on the cheese-grater. Be careful with the sharp bits! Sprinkle the tortilla chips over a large plate, then sprinkle with the olives and peppers, and finally with the cheese.

3 Get a grownup to put the plate under the broiler, and broil until the cheese has melted. You're done! Be careful with the plate though as it will be really hot.

Snack on a Stick

Feeds 4

Snacks you can eat on the move.

You'll need:
A plastic serrated knife
A spoon
A chopping board
Some wooden skewers

Ingredients

1 yellow bell pepper

1 red bell pepper

1 zucchini

12 cherry tomatoes

12 button mushrooms

Basil leaves

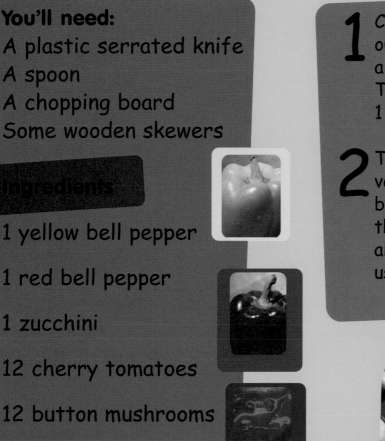

1 Cut the peppers in half and scrape out the seeds and white parts with a spoon. Slice into 1 inch squares. Then chop the zucchini into 1 inch chunks.

2 Take a skewer and push some vegetables on it, alternating between the different types. Do this with the other skewers until all the vegetables have been used up.

Extras!
Try cooking the skewers of vegetables! First, soak the skewers in cold water for 30 minutes before you add the vegetables to stop them burning, then brush them with a little olive oil. Get a grownup to broil them or grill them on the barbecue. They will be cooked when the vegetables start to blacken at the edges.

Burger Faces

Makes 4

Cheer up boring hamburgers with these funny faces!

You'll need:
A large mixing bowl
A wooden spoon
A cookie sheet
A plastic serrated knife
A chopping board

Ingredients

For the burgers:
1lb 2oz (4¼ cups)
  ground beef
1 small onion, minced
½ cup fresh bread crumbs
2 free-range eggs, beaten
1 tablespoon Worcestershire
  sauce
1 tablespoon ketchup
Oil for greasing
2 hamburger buns

To decorate:
Iceberg lettuce leaves
Cherry tomatoes, halved
Slices of dill pickle
Slice of cheese
1 tube processed cheese spread
A few black peppercorns

1 Preheat the oven to 400°F. Put all of the ingredients for the burgers in a mixing bowl and mix well. Oil the cookie sheet.

2 With wet hands, divide the mixture into 4, then flatten into patties, and place on the oiled cookie sheet.

3 Get a grownup to bake them for 12 to 15 minutes. The patties need to be turned over halfway through cooking.

4 Check the center of one hamburger to make sure it's cooked through – it shouldn't be red in the center. Transfer the cooked hamburgers to kitchen paper to absorb the grease.

5 Put a lettuce leaf on one half of a burger bun, then place a burger on top.

6 Now comes the fun part — decorating the burger. You can do whatever you like. Be creative!

7 To make the burgers look like those in the picture, put half a cherry tomato in the center of the burgers for a nose, then squeeze 2 dots of processed cheese on each for the eyes, and draw on a mouth. Squash a thin slice of pickle above the eyes and then put a peppercorn in the center of each face. Don't eat the peppercorns though–they're hot!

Extras!
Make them for your friends and family and let them decorate their own burgers.

You can use other foods to decorate your faces, such as beets, olives, mushrooms, ham, tomato ketchup, corn kernels, and so on.

Pasta Spirals and Stars

Feeds 4

This is a great dish to make, because you get to be head chef and tell a grownup what to do!

You'll need:
A plastic serrated knife
A chopping board
A vegetable peeler
A small star-shaped
  cookie-cutter
2 large saucepans
A colander
An apron
A wooden spoon

Ingredients

1 large sweet potato
1 large zucchini
1 cup snowpeas
1 small head of broccoli
2 tomatoes
1 garlic clove
$1/2$ cup bean sprouts
2 teaspoons salt
9oz dried pasta
  spirals (fusilli)
3 tablespoons olive oil

1 First peel the sweet potato and get a grownup to slice it lengthwise into $1/4$ inch slices. Then get your cookie-cutter and cut the slices into star shapes on the chopping board. Chop the zucchini into $1/2$ inch pieces. Slice the snowpeas in half and break the broccoli into florets (those are the individual flowery bits).

2 Peel and finely chop the garlic and cut the tomatoes in half. Scoop out the seeds and chop into little pieces. Get a grownup to fill the saucepans with water, add a teaspoon of salt to each, and then bring to the boil. Be careful not to touch them as boiling water is very dangerous!

3 Now you get to boss the grownup about! Get them to cook the pasta for you in one of the pans and then drain it in the colander.

4 Next, ask them to add the sweet potato stars to the other pan of water and boil them for 5 minutes. Then get them to add the snowpeas, zucchini, and broccoli to the water Cook for another 3 minutes and then drain the vegetables and add them to the pasta.

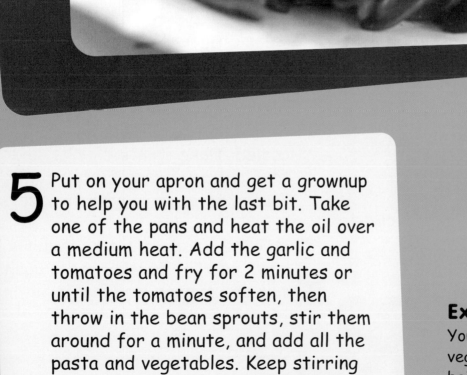

5 Put on your apron and get a grownup to help you with the last bit. Take one of the pans and heat the oil over a medium heat. Add the garlic and tomatoes and fry for 2 minutes or until the tomatoes soften, then throw in the bean sprouts, stir them around for a minute, and add all the pasta and vegetables. Keep stirring until everything has mixed together and it's all hot. To serve, divide the mixture between 4 plates.

Extras!

You can use lots of different vegetables in this pasta, try boiling pieces of carrot, green beans, or peas, or frying thinly sliced bell peppers, mushrooms, and onions.

Goldfish and Fries

Feeds 4

You'll need:
A vegetable peeler
A plastic serrated knife
A saucepan
A potato masher
A mixing bowl
A fork
3 shallow bowls
A skillet
A roasting pan

Ingredients

For the goldfish cakes:
9oz potatoes
2 tablespoons butter
9oz white fish
 (cod, snapper, grouper, etc.)
1 tablespoon minced parsley
Salt and black pepper
3 tablespoons all-purpose flour
1 free-range egg, beaten
$^2/_3$ cup fresh bread crumbs
Olive oil

For the French fries:
4 large potatoes
1-2 tablespoons sunflower oil

1 To make the goldfish cakes, peel the potatoes with the vegetable peeler, being careful with the sharp edge, and then slice them into large chunks. Ask a grownup to put the potatoes in the saucepan with enough water to cover, and to boil the potatoes for 15 minutes, then drain them. When they have cooled, mash them with the masher, then add the butter and mash them again.

2 Next, ask a grownup to put the fish in a saucepan of boiling water and simmer it for 8 minutes (simmer means cook it on a low heat so it's just bubbling). After it's cooked, get the grownup to remove the fish from the pan, put it on a plate and, when it has cooled, flake it into chunks, and take out any bones that are left. This is often done with tweezers.

3 Mix the potato and fish in a mixing bowl, add the parsley and a dash of salt and pepper, and mix it all together.

4 Wet your hands, divide the mixture into 4, and then mold each piece into a fish shape. When they are finished, refrigerate them for 20 to 30 minutes to firm up.

5 Now take 3 small, shallow bowls and put the flour in one, the egg in the next, and the bread crumbs in the last. To coat the fish, first roll them in the flour, tapping off the excess, then coat in the egg, and finally coat in the bread crumbs, pressing the crumbs on firmly so they stick.

6 Now ask a grownup to shallow-fry them for you in olive oil for 4 to 5 minutes on each side, or until they are golden-brown.

7 To make the French fries, preheat the oven to 425°F. Peel the potatoes with the vegetable peeler, and slice them into long pieces about $1/4$ inch thick. Put them in a roasting pan. Pour the oil over the French fries and mix them around so they are coated.

8 Ask a grownup to cook them in the oven for 15 minutes, giving them a shake halfway through, until they are golden-brown.

Extras!
Try adding 4 minced scallions or 4 slices chopped cooked bacon to the potato mixture. Also try making the French fries from sweet potatoes or pumpkin.

Pizza-making fun for the family

Makes 4 pizzas

If you're cooking for the family or have friends over, make the dough yourself and let everyone have fun adding their own toppings.

You'll need:
A food processor
1 large mixing bowl
1 rolling pin
4 baking trays (if you want to cook all of them at once)

Dough:
6 cups all-purpose flour
1 package dry yeast
2 teaspoons salt
1 teaspoons sugar
1¼ cups warm water

Tomato topping:
1 x 14oz can chopped tomatoes
2 garlic cloves, minced
1 tablespoon dried oregano
1 teaspoon sugar
3 tablespoons olive oil

To make the dough

1 Put the flour, yeast, salt, and sugar together in a food processor. Get a grownup to help you with this.

2 Turn to medium speed and start to slowly pour in the water until all of it has been added. When the mixture forms a big ball, dust a work surface with flour, and tip the dough onto it.

3 Now for the fun bit — kneading! Basically, you've got to push, roll, stretch, and fold the dough over and over again until it feels smooth and stretchy. This will take around 3 to 5 minutes.

4 Now put your dough in a clean bowl and cover it with a damp kitchen towel. Leave for about 1 to 1½ hours or until it has doubled in size.

5 Turn the oven on as hot as it goes (450°F) and then start making the tomato topping. Put the tomatoes, garlic, oregano, sugar, and oil in a bowl and mash them with a fork until they're mushy.

6 Now take your dough and give it a punch in the center to knock the air out of it. Then cut into 4 pieces. Roll each piece into squares or circles ¼ inch thick and place on a floured baking tray. Spread 2 to 3 tablespoons of topping over each pizza, leaving a space around the edge for the crust, then add the toppings.

Toppings

Everyone likes different things on their pizzas. Here are some ideas to get you started. Oh, and remember that in Italy, where pizza comes from, they don't use too many toppings because they make the pizza go soggy and then it doesn't taste as good!

Cheese: cubes of fresh mozzarella (it goes stringy when it's cooked) or grated yellow cheese.
Meat: ham, pepperoni, chicken, broiled or fried bacon.
Vegetables: bell peppers, mushrooms, olives, tomatoes, zucchini, spinach.

Ask a grownup to bake your pizzas in the oven for 7 to 10 minutes, or until the crust is golden and the cheese has melted.

Fajitas

Feeds 4

You'll need:
A serrated plastic knife
A spoon
A chopping board
A mixing bowl
A roasting pan

Ingredients

1 Bermuda onion

1 red bell pepper

1 yellow bell pepper

4 skinless chicken breasts

3 tablespoons olive oil

1 lime, juice squeezed

1 teaspoon powdered cumin

1 teaspoon smoked paprika

1 teaspoon oregano

1 avocado

Eight 10-inch flour tortillas

Sour cream, grated Monterey Jack cheese, salsa, and jalapeño peppers to serve

1 Preheat the oven to: 400°F.

2 Cut the peppers in half, scrape out the seeds and white parts with a spoon, and slice into strips. Peel the onion and slice that too. Next cut the chicken into 1/2 inch strips and put it in the bowl with the onions.

3 Mix the oil, lime juice, cumin, paprika, and oregano in a bowl. Pour the mixture over the chicken and vegetables and mix together until everything is coated.

4 Pour everything in a roasting pan and get a grownup to put it in the oven for 12 minutes. Ask the grownup to give the pan a shake halfway through the cooking time. While everything is in the oven, peel and chop the avocado. A real easy way to do this it to cut it around the center from top to bottom, remove the pit, then put the edge of a big spoon between the skin and the flesh, and scoop it out.

5 When the chicken is cooked, it shouldn't be pink in the center. Get a grownup to put it on a plate, and put it on a table with the avocado, tortillas, and everything else.

6 Get everyone to make their own fajitas, putting a little of everything on a tortilla and rolling it up.

Extras!

Try adding other vegetables to your fajitas, such as a sliced zucchini, and some sliced mushrooms. Or why not try sprinkling a tablespoon or 2 of chopped cilantro leaves over the chicken and vegetables before serving for a fresh herb taste?

Greek Salad

Serves 4

This is a quick and tasty salad recipe, which is eaten all over Greece.

You'll need:
A serrated plastic knife
A chopping board
A large mixing bowl
A jelly glass (with lid)

Ingredients

For the salad:
1 iceberg lettuce
6 tomatoes
1 medium cucumber
1 cup feta cheese
16 black olives,
   pitted and halved

For the dressing:
3 tablespoons olive oil
1 tablespoon lemon juice
1 teaspoon Dijon-style mustard
1 teaspoon oregano
A dash black pepper

1 First shred the lettuce, then chop the tomatoes, cucumber, and feta into big chunks and put them all in a large bowl with the olives.

2 To make the dressing, put the olive oil, lemon juice, mustard, oregano, and a dash of pepper in the jelly glass, and screw on the lid tightly.

3 When you're ready to serve the salad, shake the dressing in the jar until it's all mixed up, then pour it over the salad and toss everything lightly so the salad is coated with the dressing.

4 Bring it to the table and let everyone help themselves.

Extras!
Try adding half a sliced Bermuda onion or 2 tablespoons fresh minced parsley or mint leaves to your salad.

Chicken Skewers

Feeds 4

Impress your family by making these delicious kabobs.

You'll need:
A plastic serrated knife
A chopping board
A spoon
A juicer
Some skewers soaked
 in cold water

Ingredients

1 Bermuda onion

2 red bell peppers

4 skinless chicken breasts

$1/3$ cup olive oil

1 teaspoon paprika

2 garlic cloves, minced

Juice of 1 lime

1 Carefully peel the onion with a plastic knife and chop into 1 inch chunks, then cut the pepper in half and scrape out the seeds and white parts with a spoon. Chop into pieces the same size as the onion, then do the same with the chicken.

2 Mix the oil, paprika, garlic, and lime juice together in a bowl and stir in the chicken. Put them into the refrigerator for 1 hour to marinate, and let the flavors combine.

3 When you are ready to cook, push alternate pieces of chicken and vegetable onto the skewers until they are used up.

4 Get a grownup to cook the skewers under a hot broiler, or on a grill or barbecue, for 7 to 10 minutes. Check to see if they are cooked inside by cutting the thickest piece of chicken, there shouldn't be any pink inside.

Extras!
Try adding zucchini, mushrooms and cherry tomatoes, and add extra herbs and spices to the marinade such as oregano, or cumin.

Tomato Soup

Feeds 4

You'll need:
An apron
A plastic serrated knife
A chopping board
A large saucepan
A blender

Ingredients

1 large onion

1 tablespoon olive oil

1 x 14oz can plum
tomatoes, chopped

1 tablespoon tomato paste

A bunch of basil leaves
(about 4oz)

2½ cups vegetable broth

½ teaspoon salt

½ teaspoon black pepper

Basil leaves to decorate

1 Wearing an apron, first peel and thinly slice the onion. Then get a grownup to help you with the cooking. The saucepan and soup will be very hot, so never try this on your own.

2 Put the oil and the onion in the saucepan, stir them, and then cook on a low heat for 10 minutes or until the onions are soft.

3 Add the rest of the ingredients and simmer (that means cook so it's barely bubbling) for 30 minutes, stirring from time to time.

4 Let the mixture cool down a little and then get a grownup to help with the next part. Carefully pour the mixture into the blender, put on the lid and hold it down. Blend until the mixture is really smooth, then pour it back into the saucepan. Warm it up just until it's hot and serve it with some nice, crusty bread. Decorate with a few basil leaves.

Extras!
Try stirring 3 tablespoons of light or heavy cream into the soup when you warm it up at the end. This will make it cream of tomato soup.

Mixed Green Salad with Chicken and Bacon

Feeds 4

This is a great dish for all the family.

You'll need:
A chopping board
A plastic serrated knife
A large mixing bowl
A jelly glass (with lid)

Ingredients

For the salad:
1 small lettuce
1 cucumber
6 tomatoes
$^1/_2$ Bermuda onion
1 bell pepper
2 cooked chicken breasts
8 slices broiled or fried bacon

For the dressing:
5 tablespoons olive oil
2 tablespoons fresh lemon juice
2 tablespoons Dijon-style mustard
1 tablespoon liquid honey

1 Take a chopping board and chop all of the ingredients into pieces that are all the same size. Put them into a mixing bowl.

2 To make the dressing, put the dressing ingredients into the jelly glass and screw the lid on tightly.

3 When you are ready to eat the salad, give the dressing a really good shake so it's all mixed up, then pour it over the salad. Give it all a good mix so everything is coated in the dressing, then take it to the table, and let everyone serve themselves.

Extras!
Try using different types of vegetables or salad leaves in your salad, such as zucchini, scallions, arugula, and alfalfa sprouts. You can exchange the chicken and bacon for cubes of cheese, ham, or tuna. Experiment and see which one you like best.

Halloween Pumpkin Soup

Feeds 6-8

This is a really cool soup to make for a Halloween party!
Serve it in a pumpkin head.

You'll need:
A large saucepan
An apron
A serrated knife
A chopping board

Ingredients

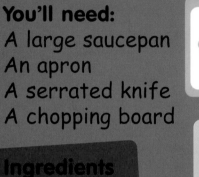

1 large pumpkin (around 3lb), to produce about $1^1/_2$lb flesh

2 tablespoons olive oil

1 large onion, minced

2 garlic cloves, minced

2 teaspoons ground cumin

2 teaspoons sweet paprika

1 tablespoon ground coriander

$2^1/_4$ cups vegetable broth

$2^1/_4$ cups milk

1 teaspoon salt

$^1/_2$teaspoon black pepper

1 First ask a grownup to help you hollow out the pumpkin. Ask them to cut a large hole in the top for you, then scrape out the seeds and throw them away (or dry them, sprinkle with a little salt, and eat them later). Now scrape out the orange flesh, being careful not to break through the skin of the pumpkin.

2 Put on your apron and get a grownup to help you with the cooking. The saucepan and soup will be very hot, so never try this by yourself.

3 Heat the oil in the saucepan, and add the onion and garlic. Stir well. Reduce the heat and cook on a low heat for 10 minutes, or until the onions are soft.

4 Add the spices and stir for 2 to 3 minutes before adding the rest of the ingredients, including the pumpkin flesh. Simmer (that means cook so it's barely bubbling) for 30 minutes, stirring from time to time.

5 Let the mixture cool down for about 20 minutes, then get a grownup to help with the next part. Carefully pour the mixture into the blender, put on the lid and hold it down, covered with a kitchen towel. Whiz it up until it's really smooth; there's lots of soup so you may have to do this in 2 or 3 batches.

6 Pour the liquid back into the saucepan, warm it up, and serve it with some garlic bread to scare off the vampires!

Extras!

To serve it in a pumpkin head, draw a scary face on the pumpkin with a magic marker. Put the head in a preheated 300°F oven for 10 to 15 minutes to warm it up, before pouring your soup inside.

Sprinkle the soup with lots of chopped parsley before serving. Make some garlic toast, and cut it into interesting shapes, such as stars and moons, using a cookie cutter.

Easter Bunny Cookies

Makes 16-20

You'll need:
A mixing bowl
A wooden spoon
A rabbit-shaped
  cookie cutter
A metal spatula
A baking tray
A wire cooling rack

Ingredients

3 cups self-rising flour

A dash of salt

1 cup butter, chilled,
  cut in cubes

$1/2$ cup superfine sugar

Decoration:
Chocolate chips or
  green ball sprinkles
  for the eyes

1 Preheat the oven to 400°F. Put the flour, salt, and butter in a mixing bowl and rub it together with your fingertips until it looks like bread crumbs.

2 Add the sugar and stir the mixture until it forms a dough.

3 Dust a work surface and rolling pin with a little flour and roll out the dough until it is $1/2$ inch thick.

4 Grease the baking tray with a little butter, then cut out bunny shapes with the cookie cutter and transfer them to the tray using the metal spatula. Put a chocolate chip or green ball on each cookie for an eye.

5 Ask a grownup to bake them in the oven for 15 to 20 minutes or until golden. Then ask the grownup to arrange them on a wire cooling rack, and leave them to cool.

Birthday Cake

Celebrating a birthday in the family with a homemade cake is far more personal and special than a storebought one.

You'll need:

2 x 7-inch shallow cake pans
Scissors
Some nonstick baking paper
A large mixing bowl
A wooden spoon
A metal spatula
A skewer
A wire cooling rack

Birthday candles, as many as the person's age.

Ingredients

$^3/_4$ cup softened butter
$^3/_4$ cup superfine sugar
3 medium free-range eggs
1 teaspoon vanilla extract
$1^1/_2$ cups self-rising flour
1 teaspoon baking powder

For decoration:

5-6 tablespoons apricot jelly
$^1/_3$ cup unsalted butter
$1^1/_2$ cups confectioner's sugar
3 drops vanilla extract
Sprinkles or other cake decorations

1 First grease and line the cake pans. Place 1 pan on 2 sheets of nonstick baking paper and draw round it, then cut out the circles. Grease the inside of the pans with butter and then put the paper circles in the bottom.

2 Preheat the oven to 375°F. Put the sugar and butter in a mixing bowl and beat together until creamy. Add the eggs and vanilla extract and beat again until the mixture is smooth.

3 Sift the flour into a bowl. Then add it into the mixture and mix well.

4 Divide the mixture between the 2 pans and smooth the top with a metal spatula. Ask a grownup to bake them in the center of the oven for about 20 minutes, or until risen and golden on top. Test to see if the cakes are done by pushing a wooden skewer in the center of the cakes. If it comes out clean then they're ready.

5 Leave the cakes to cool for 5 minutes then take them out of their pans and put them onto the wire rack. When they are completely cool, ask a grownup to slice them into 3 layers across the center with a sharp knife.

6 Spread 2 tablespoons apricot jelly on 3 of the slices of cake. Arrange them on top of each other, with the layer without jelly on the top.

7 To make the frosting, put the butter and confectioner's sugar into a bowl and beat until creamy. Add the vanilla extract and 1 tablespoon water. Beat until the mixture is smooth, thick, and spreadable. If it's too thick, add another tablespoon of water.

8 Spread the frosting all over the cake with a metal spatula and then add sprinkles or other cake decorations.

Extras!
For a chocolate cake, add 2 tablespoons unsweetened cocoa powder to the flour. For the frosting, add 1 tablespoon unsweetened cocoa powder and an extra tablespoon of water to the mixture.

Bat Cookies

Makes 10–12

These cool cookies are just right for a Halloween party!

You'll need:
A large mixing bowl
A small bowl
A sieve
A wooden spoon
A piping bag or a
   small plastic freezer bag
A rolling pin
A bat-shaped
   cookie cutter
A chopping board
A cookie sheet
A wire cooling rack

Ingredients

For the cookies:
$^1/_2$ cup superfine sugar
1 stick softened butter,
   plus more for greasing
the cookie sheet
1 free-range egg, beaten
2 drops vanilla extract
2 cups all-purpose flour,
   plus more for dusting

For the frosting:
2 scant cups confectioner's sugar
Black food coloring
Orange food coloring

1 Preheat the oven to 375°F. Put the sugar and butter in a large mixing bowl and beat together until creamy.

2 Add the egg and vanilla extract and keep beating until the mixture is smooth. Now stir in the flour, a little at a time, until you have a smooth dough.

3 Dust the chopping board and rolling pin with a little flour and roll the dough out until it's about $^1/_4$ inch thick. Dust with more flour if it sticks to the board.

4 Grease a cookie sheet with butter. Then use a cookie cutter to cut out cookies. Put the cookies on the cookie sheet. If there are some scraps of dough left over, bake them too, you can eat them later as a treat for your hard work!

5 Get a grownup to put the cookie sheet in the center of the oven and bake for 10 minutes. When ready, get the grownup to transfer the cookies to a wire rack to cool.

6 To make the frosting, sift the confectioner's sugar into a bowl and add a tablespoon of water. Mix with a wooden or plastic spoon.

7 Take 3 tablespoons of the frosting and put it in a small bowl. Add a few drops of orange food coloring to make it bright orange. Add black food coloring to the rest of the frosting.

8 Spread the black frosting over the cookies with a metal spatula. Put the orange frosting in a piping bag or a freezer bag with the corner snipped off. Draw lines down the wings and make little dots for eyes.

Extras!

You can easily use the same cookie mixture for Christmas cookies. Use a Christmas tree cookie cutter to get the right shape and spread the cookie with green frosting. Dot with white frosting for the tree decorations.

Spider Web Cakes

Perfect cakes for Halloween!

You'll need:
A large mixing bowl
A wooden spoon
Sieve
A 16-cup muffin pan
   or 16 cupcake cases
A wire cooling rack
Plastic freezer bag
A cocktail stick

Ingredients

$1/2$ cup superfine sugar
$1/2$ cup butter, softened
2 free-range eggs, beaten
1 cup self-rising flour
$1/4$ cup golden raisins

For the frosting:
$2/3$ cup confectioner's
   sugar
A few drops of brown
   food coloring

1 Preheat the oven to 375°F. Put the sugar and butter in a mixing bowl and beat until they are creamy. Now add the eggs and beat again until the mixture is smooth.

2 Next, sift the flour into the bowl. This gets air into the flour and makes the cakes fluffier. When all the flour is in the bowl, stir it into the mixture and then mix in the golden raisins. They are the dead flies in your spider web cakes!

3 Divide the mixture between the muffin cups or the cake-cases and ask a grownup to bake them in the oven for 15 to 20 minutes, or until they've risen and are golden. Then ask the grownup to put them on a wire rack to cool.

4 Meanwhile, make the frosting. Sift the confectioner's sugar into a small bowl and add 1 tablespoon of water. Mix it together until it forms a thick smooth paste, adding a little more water if you need to. Take 4 tablespoons of the frosting and put it in another bowl.

5 Mix in the food coloring, a few drops at a time, until the frosting is dark brown.

6 When the cakes are cool, spread the white frosting over the tops of the cakes. Now take a plastic freezer bag and cut off the tip of one corner. Spoon in the brown frosting and then draw circles on the tops of the cakes, starting small and making bigger and bigger circles until you reach the edge.

7 When you have covered all the cakes, take a cocktail stick and pull it through the circles from the inside to the edge, about 6 or 7 times on each cake, so it looks like a spider's web.

Extras!

You can swap the golden raisins for the same amount of chocolate chips if you like. You can also try using different food colorings and draw pictures or names on top of your cakes.

Index